Guthrie

by Iain Gray

WRITING *to* REMEMBER

79 Main Street, Newtongrange,
Midlothian EH22 4NA
Tel: 0131 344 0414
E-mail: info@lang-syne.co.uk
www.langsyneshop.co.uk

Design by Dorothy Meikle
Printed by Printwell Ltd
© Lang Syne Publishers Ltd 2024

All rights reserved. No part of this publication may be reproduced, stored or introduced into a retrieval system, or transmitted in any form or by any means (electronic, mechanical, photocopying, recording or otherwise) without the prior written permission of Lang Syne Publishers Ltd.

ISBN 978-1-85217-760-7

Guthrie

MOTTO:
I stand for truth

CREST:
An embowed arm,
the hand grasping a sword

TERRITORY:
Angus

NAME variations include:
 Guthere
 Guttrie
 Guthree

Chapter one:

The origins of the clan system

by Rennie McOwan

The original Scottish clans of the Highlands and the great families of the Lowlands and Borders were gatherings of families, relatives, allies and neighbours for mutual protection against rivals or invaders.

Scotland experienced invasion from the Vikings, the Romans and English armies from the south. The Norman invasion of what is now England also had an influence on land-holding in Scotland. Some of these invaders stayed on and in time became 'Scottish'.

The word clan derives from the Gaelic language term 'clann', meaning children, and it was first used many centuries ago as communities were formed around tribal lands in glens and mountain fastnesses.

The format of clans changed over the centuries, but at its best the chief and his family held the land on behalf of all, like trustees, and the ordinary clansmen and women believed they had a blood relationship with the founder of their clan.

There were two way duties and obligations. An inadequate chief could be deposed and replaced by someone of greater ability.

Clan people had an immense pride in race. Their relationship with the chief was like adult children to a father and they had a real dignity.

The concept of clanship is very old and a more feudal notion of authority gradually crept in.

Pictland, for instance, was divided into seven principalities ruled by feudal leaders who were the strongest and most charismatic leaders of their particular groups.

By the sixth century the 'British' kingdoms of Strathclyde, Lothian and Celtic Dalriada (Argyll) had emerged and Scotland, as one nation, began to take shape in the time of King Kenneth MacAlpin.

Some chiefs claimed descent from ancient kings which may not have been accurate in every case.

By the twelfth and thirteenth centuries the clans and families were more strongly brought under the central control of Scottish monarchs.

Lands were awarded and administered more and more under royal favour, yet the power of the area clan chiefs was still very great.

The long wars to ensure Scotland's

independence against the expansionist ideas of English monarchs extended the influence of some clans and reduced the lands of others.

Those who supported Scotland's greatest king, Robert the Bruce, were awarded the territories of the families who had opposed his claim to the Scottish throne.

In the Scottish Borders country – the notorious Debatable Lands – the great families built up a ferocious reputation for providing warlike men accustomed to raiding into England and occasionally fighting one another.

Chiefs had the power to dispense justice and to confiscate lands and clan warfare produced a society where martial virtues – courage, hardiness, tenacity – were greatly admired.

Gradually the relationship between the clans and the Crown became strained as Scottish monarchs became more orientated to life in the Lowlands and, on occasion, towards England.

The Highland clans spoke a different language, Gaelic, whereas the language of Lowland Scotland and the court was Scots and in more modern times, English.

Highlanders dressed differently, had different

customs, and their wild mountain land sometimes seemed almost foreign to people living in the Lowlands.

It must be emphasised that Gaelic culture was very rich and story-telling, poetry, piping, the clarsach (harp) and other music all flourished and were greatly respected.

Highland culture was different from other parts of Scotland but it was not inferior or less sophisticated.

Central Government, whether in London or Edinburgh, sometimes saw the Gaelic clans as a challenge to their authority and some sent expeditions into the Highlands and west to crush the power of the Lords of the Isles.

Nevertheless, when the eighteenth century Jacobite Risings came along the cause of the Stuarts was mainly supported by Highland clans.

The word Jacobite comes from the Latin for James – Jacobus. The Jacobites wanted to restore the exiled Stuarts to the throne of Britain.

The monarchies of Scotland and England became one in 1603 when King James VI of Scotland (1st of England) gained the English throne after Queen Elizabeth died.

The Union of Parliaments of Scotland and England, the Treaty of Union, took place in 1707.

Some Highland clans, of course, and Lowland families opposed the Jacobites and supported the incoming Hanoverians.

After the Jacobite cause finally went down at Culloden in 1746 a kind of ethnic cleansing took place. The power of the chiefs was curtailed. Tartan and the pipes were banned in law.

Many emigrated, some because they wanted to, some because they were evicted by force. In addition, many Highlanders left for the cities of the south to seek work.

Many of the clan lands became home to sheep and deer shooting estates.

But the warlike traditions of the clans and the great Lowland and Border families lived on, with their descendants fighting bravely for freedom in two world wars.

Remember the men from whence you came, says the Gaelic proverb, and to that could be added the role of many heroic women.

The spirit of the clan, of having roots, whether Highland or Lowland, means much to thousands of people.

Meanwhile, many families proudly boast the heraldic device known as a Coat of Arms,.

The central motif of the Coat of Arms would originally have been what was sometimes borne on the shield of a warrior to distinguish himself from others on the battlefield.

Clan warfare produced a society where courage and tenacity were greatly admired

Chapter two:

In freedom's cause

A locational, or habitational, surname, 'Guthrie' is identified with the lands of the name in Angus, in the northeast of Scotland.

Located near Forfar, the Guthrie place name derives from the Gaelic *gaothair*, meaning 'windy place', while another suggestion as to its origin is that it is an Anglicisation of the Irish-Gaelic surname *O'Fhlaitheamh*, indicating 'descendant of Flaitheamh', or from *MagUchtre*, denoting 'son of Uchrtre'.

Although interesting, one other rather fanciful theory is that the lands of Guthrie were so named by an early, and very hungry, king after he got a local fisherman to *gut three* fish to feed him – with 'gut three' a homonym for 'Guthrie'.

The lands from which Clan Guthrie takes its name and on which they were employed as falconers at an early date, were the property of the Crown until about 1178 when King William I, better known as William the Lyon, gifted them to Arbroath Abbey.

Jumping slightly ahead in the historical timeline of the clan, it was during the reign from 1329 to 1371 of King David II that they were granted the Barony of Guthrie, setting them on the path to become a significant force in the north-eastern reaches of the realm.

Before this, however, the clan had already enjoyed a significant degree of influence in Scottish affairs.

This is borne out by the fact that it was 'The Laird of Guthrie' – his name unfortunately now lost to posterity – who was entrusted with the important task of persuading the great freedom fighter Sir William Wallace to return from France to his native land to renew the struggle following his defeat at the battle of Falkirk in 1298.

Two years earlier, a humiliating treaty of fealty to England's conquering King Edward I, known as the Hammer of the Scots, had been signed at Berwick by 1,500 Scottish earls, bishops and burgesses – with the parchment known as the *Ragman Roll* because of the profusion of ribbons that dangled from the seals of the signatories.

Wallace raised the banner of revolt against English occupation in May of 1297 after slaying Sir William Heselrig, Sheriff of Lanark, apparently in revenge for killing his young wife, Marion.

Proving an expert in the tactics of guerrilla warfare, Wallace and his hardened band of freedom fighters inflicted stunning defeats on a number of English garrisons, culminating in the liberation of practically all of Scotland following the battle of Stirling Bridge on September 11, 1297.

The army led by Wallace and his fellow commander Sir Andrew Moray – with Guthries in all likelihood in the ranks of the latter, had met up and

prepared to meet a mighty English army of invasion that had hurriedly been despatched north by Edward I.

Despite a complement of only 8,000 foot soldiers and 36 cavalry, compared to the army under the Earl of Surrey that boasted no less than 10,000 foot soldiers and 200 knights, the Scots held a strategic advantage that they exploited to the full.

Positioning their army on the heights of Abbey Craig, on the outskirts of Stirling and where the imposing Wallace Monument now stands, the Scots commanders waited patiently as Essex's force ponderously made its way across a narrow bridge spanning the waters of the Forth.

As the bulk of the army crossed from the bridge onto the marshy ground at the foot of Abbey Craig, the piercing blast of a hunting horn signalled a ferocious charge down the hillside of massed ranks of spearmen.

Trapped on the boggy ground, the English were incapable of putting up effective resistance. They were hacked to death in their hundreds, while many others drowned in their heavy armour in the swirling waters of the Forth as they attempted to make their way back across the bridge.

The Scots celebrated a great victory and

both Wallace – who was subsequently knighted – and Moray were appointed joint Guardians of Scotland, but a crushing defeat came less than a year later, in April of 1298 at the battle of Falkirk – in large part due to the deadly fusillades of fire from the Welsh bowmen in the ranks of the English army.

Wallace escaped the battlefield and, in September, resigned his guardianship in favour of Robert Bruce, the future king destined to be the victor of the battle of Bannockburn in 1314.

Wallace's movements are now unclear, but there is evidence he embarked on a mission to France at some stage to the court of King Philip IV to enlist French aid in Scotland's cause.

Later the Laird of Guthrie travelled to France, authorised by a number of Scotland's leading nobles to invite Wallace back and renew the struggle.

Mission accomplished the pair landed safely at Montrose and Wallace wasted no time in organising a series of attacks on English garrisons.

But, after being betrayed, he was captured in August of 1305 and dragged off to London in chains, where he was tried and found guilty of the ludicrous charge of treason against Edward I.

His end was truly horrific.

Stripped naked, he was dragged through London at the heels of a horse to the place of execution at Smithfield.

Strangled by hanging but cut down while still alive, he was emasculated, eviscerated, his bowels burned before his eyes, beheaded and his body cut into quarters.

Unveiled more than 650 years later, in 1956, a plaque near the site of his execution reads, translated from Latin:

I tell you the truth. Freedom is what is best.
Sons, never live like slaves.

Just over 140 years after Wallace's execution, the Laird of Guthrie's descendant, Alexander Guthrie of Guthrie, added to the clan's territories by acquiring the lands of Kincaldrum, near Forfar, thereby becoming Baillie of Forfar, while in 1461 Sir David Guthrie of Guthrie, armour bearer to the king, was appointed Lord Treasurer of Scotland.

Gaining further royal trust and favour, in 1473 Sir David, who also founded a collegiate church at Guthrie, was appointed Lord Chief Justice of Scotland while, five years earlier, he had been granted a charter under King James II to build Guthrie Castle, near Forfar.

Originally consisting of only a square tower a formidable fourteen feet thick, and where the family lived, a house was built nearby in about 1760; this was connected to the tower in 1848, while major renovations were carried out in the following decade.

In private hands since 1984, the castle is now a popular northeast venue for weddings and other special events.

Other Guthrie properties, or former properties, include Gagie House, near Dundee, built in 1614 and which served for a time as the dower house for the laird's eldest son.

Now privately owned, it is home to a number of family portraits that once graced Guthrie Castle and which were bought by the Friends of Guthrie Castle when the castle was sold.

Including an estate of more than 12,000 acres, Torosay Castle on the Isle of Mull was bought by the wealthy London businessman Arbuthnot Charles Guthrie in 1865 and sold to the McLean Fund in 2012.

Meanwhile, spending his time between the United Kingdom and Italy, at the time of writing the Chief of Clan Guthrie is Alexander Guthrie of Guthrie 22nd of that Ilk.

Chapter three:

Bible and sword

In common with many other Scottish clans, along with their Irish counterparts, when not engaged in battling a common enemy such as an English army, they found an outlet for their martial passions through fighting with one another.

In the case of Clan Guthrie, this was with their neighbours Clan Gardyne, and in 1578 Patrick Gardyne of that Ilk was killed by William Guthrie – sparking off a feud that led to many casualties on both sides.

The circumstances surrounding the slaying of Gardyne were hotly disputed, and the feud was not finally resolved until 1618 through what appears to have been the intervention of the Crown.

Just over 100 years before this inter-clan feud was resolved, on September 9, 1513 Sir Alexander Guthrie, one of his sons and three of his brothers-in-law were among the 5,000 Scots including James IV, an archbishop, two bishops, eleven earls, fifteen barons, and 300 knights killed at the battle of Flodden.

The Scottish monarch had embarked on the venture after Queen Anne of France, under the terms of the Auld Alliance between Scotland and her nation, appealed to him to 'break a lance' on her behalf and act as her chosen knight.

Crossing the border at the head of a 25,000-strong army that included 7,500 clansmen and their kinsmen, James engaged a 20,000-strong force commanded by the Earl of Surrey.

Despite their numerical superiority and bravery, however, the Scots proved no match for the skilled English artillery and superior military tactics of Surrey.

The tumultuous seventeenth century saw prominent bearers of the Guthrie name take opposing sides in the War of the Three Kingdoms of Scotland, England and Ireland.

Also known as the British Civil Wars and of which the English Civil war formed a part, they were sparked off in Scotland during the Bishops' Wars of 1639 and 1640.

The wars had their origin in the widely unpopular attempt by King Charles I to impose uniform religious practice between the Church of England and the proudly independent Scottish Kirk, through the introduction into Scotland of the Episcopal *Book of Common Prayer*.

Flames of unrest were fuelled on Sunday, July 23, 1637 when James Hannay, Dean of Edinburgh, attempted to read from the *Book of Common Prayer* to a packed and surly congregation in St Giles Cathedral.

Incensed by this, Jenny Geddes, a local street trader threw her stool at the hapless minister's head and – translated from Jenny's Old Scots tongue – shouted:

Devil cause you colic in your stomach, false thief: dare you say the Mass in my ear!

This was the signal for a general tumult, as others joined in by lobbing their stools and rioting broke out in the streets.

In turn, this acted as a catalyst for the signing on February 28, 1638 of the *National Covenant* – a document as important to Scottish history as the equally famed *Declaration of Arbroath* of 1320.

Described as 'the glorious marriage day of the kingdom with God', the Covenant renounced Roman Catholic belief, pledged to uphold the Presbyterian religion and called for free parliaments and assemblies.

First signed at Edinburgh's Greyfriars Kirk by nobles, barons, burgesses and ministers, it was subscribed to the following day by hundreds of common folk.

Copies were made and dispatched around the nation and subscribed to by thousands more – with its adherents becoming known as Covenanters.

This led to a civil war that raged between Covenanters and Royalists in Scotland from 1638 until 1649, when Charles I was beheaded on the orders of the English Parliament – whose military arm was the New Model Army under Oliver Cromwell.

Caught up in these convulsions was John Guthrie, 11th Chief of Clan Guthrie.

His date of birth is not known, but records show he graduated from St Andrews University in 1597, was appointed to a position in Arbroath Church in the same year and, two years later, as minister of Kinnell Parish Church, in his family homeland of Angus.

A number of other appointments followed until, in 1621, he became minister of St Giles Cathedral.

His power and influence growing, in 1623 he

was appointed Bishop of Moray and later proved to be a staunch advocate of Charles I's plans to align the Scottish Kirk with the Church of England.

But, increasingly isolated in his support of the king, he was deposed from the bishopric nearly ten years after the signing of the Covenant for persistently refusing to accept its legality.

Excommunicated by the Kirk, he fortified his bishop's seat, Spynie Palace, near Elgin, but was captured in July of 1640 after the castle fell to a besieging force of Covenanters led by Colonel Robert Munro.

Imprisoned for a time in Edinburgh's Tolbooth, he later retired to his Guthrie estate, where he died in 1649.

The father of three sons and three daughters, his youngest son Andrew Guthrie enlisted in the Royalist force that was commanded in Scotland by the charismatic James Graham, 1st Marquis of Montrose, later paying dearly for this.

Although Montrose had initially supported the Covenant, his conscience later dictated that he switch sides, with his great campaigns from 1644 to 1645 known as The Year of Miracles because of his brilliant military successes.

At the battle of Inverlochy, on the west coast, on February 2, 1645 the Earl of Argyll was forced to ignominiously flee in his galley after 1,500 of his Covenanters were wiped out in a surprise attack.

What made Montrose's victory all the more notable was that his hardy forces, including Andrew Guthrie, had arrived at Inverlochy after an exhausting 36-hour march through knee-deep snow from the area of present-day Fort Augustus.

Another great victory came at the battle of Kilsyth on August 15, but defeat at Philiphaugh, near Selkirk, followed less than a month later.

Captured in the aftermath of Philiphaugh, Andrew Guthrie was taken to Edinburgh and beheaded by the Scottish version of the French guillotine known as The Maiden.

Montrose, following another defeat at the battle of Carbisdale, Ross-shire, on April 27, 1650 was finally captured after being betrayed and hanged, beheaded and his body cut into quarters just less than a month later.

Breaking with family tradition by siding with the Covenanting cause, James Guthrie, known as James 'The Martyr' Guthrie and whom Oliver Cromwell praised as 'the short man who would not bow', was the Covenanting minister born in 1612 and thought to have been a son of Guthrie of that Ilk.

A graduate of St Andrews University, he held a number of positions within the Kirk after being ordained as a minister, and it was while minister of the Church of the Holy Rood, Stirling, that in 1649 he was stripped of office because of his Covenanting stance.

This was after the Scottish Kirk had turned a full circle by lending its support to Charles II, heir to Charles I who had been executed in 1649.

Undaunted, he continued to preach and, in 1661, denied a general amnesty that followed in the wake of the Restoration of Charles II, was hanged in Edinburgh.

In the following centuries, and in different areas of conflict, bearers of the Guthrie name have maintained their proud martial tradition.

The last Chief of Clan Guthrie to live at Guthrie Castle, Lieutenant Colonel Ivan Guthrie of Guthrie, born in 1886, was a distinguished soldier of the First World War.

Commander of 4th Battalion Black Watch, he was awarded the Military Cross (MC) at the end of the conflict in 1918 and later held a number of other military posts while, from 1955 until his death in 1959 he served as Vice Lieutenant of his native Angus.

In more contemporary times, Field Marshall Charles Guthrie, born in 1938 in Chelsea, London is the highly distinguished retired British Army officer who held a number of senior military posts.

Educated at the Royal Military College, Sandhurst and commissioned into the Welsh Guards in 1959, subsequent roles included both as a troop and a squadron commander with 22 Special Air Service (SAS), Brigade Commander of 4th Armoured Brigade and, appointed in 1994, Chief of the General Staff (CIGS).

Appointed Chief of the Defence Staff (CDS) in 1997, he was responsible for advising the government on the military conduct of the Kosovo War while, following his retirement from the army in 2000, he was created a Life Peer a year later as Baron Guthrie of Craigiebank, of Craigiebank in the City of Dundee and, in 2012, promoted to the honorary rank of Field Marshall.

Chapter four:

On the world stage

Bearers of the proud name of Guthrie have achieved international fame and acclaim through a diverse range of endeavours and pursuits.

The patriarch of a dynasty of folk musicians and political activists, **Woody Guthrie** was born in 1912 in Okemah, Oklahoma.

Born Woodrow Wilson Guthrie, it was while a teenager that he learned blues and folk songs from family friends, inspiring him to pick up the guitar and, later, compose his own songs.

Aged 19 when he first married, he was forced to leave his wife and three young children to seek employment in California in the wake of the dust storms that devastated Oklahoma, during what was known as the 'Dust Bowl' period, becoming one of thousands of 'Okies' who did so.

Working on a Los Angeles radio station, he steadily gained recognition as a 'hillbilly' musician, while from 1939 to 1940 he expressed his political views and social concerns through writing columns for the communist newspaper *People's World* – although in his lifetime he was never actually a member of any communist group. His anti-fascist credentials, meanwhile, were expressed through the slogan, 'This machine kills fascists' on his guitar.

Leaving Los Angeles for New York, in 1940 he recorded the album *Dust Bowl Ballads* and subsequently acquiring the soubriquet 'The Dust Bowl Troubadour.' It was during this period he also wrote what remains to this day his most famous song, *This Land is Your Land* which, although written in 1940, was not recorded until four years later.

With the melody adapted from an old gospel song, Guthrie wrote the lyrics in response to what he felt was the 'overplaying' on radio of Irving Berlin's *God Bless America*, considering the words 'unrealistic and complacent.'

Other memorable recordings include *Oklahoma Hills*, chosen in 2001 as the official state song of Oklahoma, and *Roll on Columbia*, chosen in 1987 as the official Washington State Folk Song.

Oklahoma Hills, meanwhile, was also recorded in 1945 by his cousin **Leon Jerry 'Jack' Guthrie**, born in 1915 and who died in 1948.

A major inspiration for a veritable who's-who of singers and songwriters who include Bob Dylan,

Johnny Cash, Pete Seeger, Bruce Springsteen, Tom Paxton and Billy Bragg, Woody Guthrie died in 1967, while he is the recipient of a number of honours and awards.

An inductee of the Oklahoma Music Hall of Fame and recipient in 2000 of a Grammy Lifetime Achievement Award, he was also honoured in 1998 by the United States Postal Service as part of its Legends of American Music series of stamps, while the Woody Guthrie Foundation administers the Woody Guthrie Archives in Tulsa, Oklahoma.

Carrying on his father's legacy, **Arlo Guthrie** is the folk singer, songwriter and actor born in 1947 in Brooklyn, New York and best known for his debut song from 1967 *Alice's Restaurant Massacree*.

At 18 minutes and 38 seconds in duration and a lampoon of the draft for the Vietnam War, it also features in the film *Alice's Restaurant*.

As a political activist, he was awarded the Peace Abbey Courage of Conviction Award in 1992, while his sister **Nora Lee Guthrie**, born in California in 1950 and who, along with her brother, was born to Woody Guthrie's second wife **Marjorie Mazia Guthrie**, is a folk musician, singer and songwriter and president of the Woody Guthrie Foundation.

The youngest daughter of Arlo Guthrie, **Sarah Lee Guthrie**, born in 1979, is the musician who, along with Johnny Irion, performs as an acoustic duo.

Across the Atlantic from the United States, **Robin Guthrie**, born in Grangemouth in 1962, is the Scottish musician, songwriter and record producer who co-founded the alternative rock band Cocteau Twins.

Back on American shores **Gwen Guthrie**, born in 1950 and who died in 1999, was the American pianist, singer and songwriter who also sang backing vocals for a range of artistes including Madonna, Aretha Franklin, Billy Joel and Stevie Wonder.

Behind the recording desk, **James K.A. Guthrie**, born in 1953 in Edmonton, Middlesex is the English recording engineer and producer best known for having worked from 1978 as engineer and producer for the progressive rock band Pink Floyd.

In a much different musical genre, **James Kelley Guthrie** was the American symphony conductor, orchestra founder and newspaper proprietor born in California in 1914 and who died in 1996.

Aged only 15 when he founded the San Bernardino Community Orchestra, now the San Bernardino Symphony, conductor of the Riverside Symphony Orchestra, the Inland Empire Symphony, and owner and publisher of the *San Bernardino Sun* newspaper, he also established the Guthrie Music Rental Library.

Aimed at encouraging music performance, the library rents – at low cost – orchestra music and scores to thousands of orchestras, schools and colleges across the United States.

From music to the highly competitive world of sport, **Janet Guthrie** is the American retired professional race car driver who was the first woman to qualify and compete in the Daytona 500 and Indianapolis 500.

Born in 1938 in Iowa City, Iowa and a former aerospace engineer, she began racing professionally in 1972, competing in the Daytona 500 in 1976, finishing 12th after engine problems, and the following year in the Indianapolis 500, finishing 29th, again after engine troubles.

An inductee of the Automotive Hall of Fame, her autobiography *Janet Guthrie: A Life at Full Throttle* was published in 2005.

Back in time to the early years of the twentieth century, **Andrew Guthrie** was the professional motorcycle racer from Hawick, in the Scottish Borders.

Born in 1897 and known as 'The Flying

Scotsman', between 1934 and 1937 the former motorcycle dispatch rider during the First World War won fourteen European Grand Prix titles and six Isle of Man TT races.

It was while leading on the last lap of the 1937 German Grand Prix that he crashed while avoiding a collision, dying later in hospital from his injuries.

From sport to the creative world of the written word, **Alfred Guthrie, Jr.**, was the award-winning American novelist, historian and screenwriter best known for his Western stories.

Born in 1901 in Bedford, Indiana, his novel *The Way West* won the 1950 Pulitzer Prize for Fiction, while his screenplay for the 1953 *Shane* was nominated for an Academy Award; he died in 1991.

On British shores, **Allan Guthrie**, born Allan Buchan in Orkney in 1965, is the Scottish author, editor of crime fiction and literary agent whose novel *Two-Way Split* was nominated for the 2007 Theakston's Old Peculiar Crime Novel of the Year Award.

In the equally creative world of art, **Sir James Guthrie,** born in Greenock in 1859, was the Scottish painter noted for his portraiture.

A member of the Royal Scottish Academy, he had spent most of his life in the Scottish Borders, executing works that include *Schoolmates* and *A Hind's Daughter*; he died in 1930.

Bearers of the Guthrie name have also excelled in the sciences and medicine.

Born in 1895 in New Bloomfield, Missouri, **Mary Jane Guthrie** was the American zoologist and authority on cytology – the interpretation of cells to detect cancer and other abnormalities – noted for her pioneering work on the cytoplasm of reproductive and endocrine cells. A member of the Genetics Society of America, the American Association of Anatomists and American Association of Zoologists, she died in 1975.

Born in 1833 in Bayswater, London, **Professor Frederick Guthrie** was the physicist and chemist who was the first to report on the horrific effects of mustard gas. The founder in 1874 of the Physical Society of London, now the Institute of Physics, he died in 1886.

In the realms of religion and philanthropy, the **Very Rev. Thomas Guthrie**, one of the leaders of the Free Church of Scotland and one of the most popular preachers of his day, was born in Brechin, Angus, in 1803.

Serving as a minister in Edinburgh, he became noted not only for his preaching but also for his philanthropic work for what were known as Ragged Schools – charitable institutions catering for the educational needs of destitute children.

He died in 1873 and is honoured through a number of memorials in Edinburgh, including a statue in Princes Street, facing Castle Street.

He was the great-grandfather of **Sir William Guthrie**, the English theatrical director born in Tunbridge Wells, Kent in 1900.

Known for staging productions for the Edinburgh International Festival and instrumental in the founding of the Stratford Festival of Canada and the Guthrie Theater in Minneapolis, Minnesota, he was knighted ten years before his death in 1971.

One particularly inventive bearer of the Guthrie name was the American physician **Samuel Guthrie**, born in 1782 in Hounsfield, New York and who died in 1848.

A rural doctor in Sackets Harbor, New York, in 1831 he became the first to discover the anaesthetic chloroform, by distilling chloride of lime with alcohol in a copper barrel.

Also the inventor of a form of percussion powder and a punch lock for igniting it – thereby rendering the flintlock musket obsolete.